Packing Tools for SUCCESS
Beyond Middle School

ESSIE CHILDERS

Packing Tools for SUCCESS Beyond Middle School
© 2013 by Essie Childers

All rights are reserved. No part of this publication may be reproduced in any form or by any electronic or mechanical means, including information storage and retrieval systems, without permission in writing by the publisher, except by a reviewer who may quote brief passages in a review. For information regarding permission, contact the publisher at info@gypsyheartpress.com

These books are available at special discounts when purchased in quantity for use as premiums, promotions, fund-raising and educational use.
For inquiries and details, contact us: info@gypsyheartpress.com.

Published by Gypsy Heart Press.
Cover design by Lisa Knight at kurllygurlldesigns.com.

ISBN: 978-0-9832514-4-6

GypsyHeart
PRESS

College Station, Texas

Dedication

To my husband, Terry, who has been my rock and the strength behind this labor of love. Thank you for providing comfort, encouragement, and for listening for forty years to my anecdotes over and over.

I love you more.

Acknowledgements

This project could not have been possible without my loyal partners.

Erin Casey, my book coach and editor, has a remarkable calmness about her and has been blessed with journalist abilities. During my writing blocks, she always knew the right words to say to help me get back on track.

Lee Nell Hill, an English professor at Tyler Junior College, has been my proofreader on this and other projects. She has a keen eye and is soft spoken. Lee Nell is not a chatter box, but when she speaks, you know to listen and take notes.

Thank you both for being my cheerleaders. You have performed beyond the call of duty.

Packing Tools for SUCCESS
Beyond Middle School*

Contents

1	Foreword
3	Packing with PRIDE
7	Pack P for Personal Responsibility
11	Pack R for Respect of Yourself & Others
15	Pack I for Involvement in School & Community
19	Pack D for Determination
25	Pack E for Excellence in Academics
29	PRIDE On!
33	Journal Reflections
48	Motivational Quotes for Success
55	Contract for Academic Success
57	References
59	About the Author

*The term "middle school" will be used to refer to all middle, junior high & intermediate schools.

Foreword

Everyone can benefit from having a wise mentor. Mentors are people with both wisdom and a caring heart. Their wisdom comes from paying close attention to the lessons they learned from school and life. Their caring heart motivates them to share their wisdom with others to help them be successful.

Essie Childers, the author of this guide, is offering to be your mentor. I hope you accept her offer. If you do, you'll benefit from her wonderful advice. Plus, I think you'll enjoy reading the personal experiences and parables she shares because they make her advice easy to understand and put into action. And if you do act on the ideas in this little book, you will have a huge head start on creating a great life.

Skip Downing
Founder, On Course Workshop
Author of *On Course: Strategies for Creating Success in College and in Life*

"You can always do
more than you think
you can do."
-John Wooden

Packing with PRIDE

Dear Student,

Middle School has often been associated with a time of transition, a period of discovery, and exercising new freedoms. It is a time of developing one's self-concept, refining values, and testing authority.

It is not generally considered as a time to think about careers, high school, or college. Middle school happens to be a crucial time in your life. It is during these years that you begin to build your foundation of learning.

Your parents may have built a house, or maybe you have seen houses being built. A builder must start with a solid foundation and use the very best tools and materials. You are building on your foundation to get ready for high school. You must start with a solid foundation (your classes) and use the very best tools —PRIDE tools.

If you look at Visuwords, PRIDE means having a feeling of self-respect and personal worth. Another way to understand pride is to "do your best" at whatever you are asked to do... your very best.

PRIDE Tools

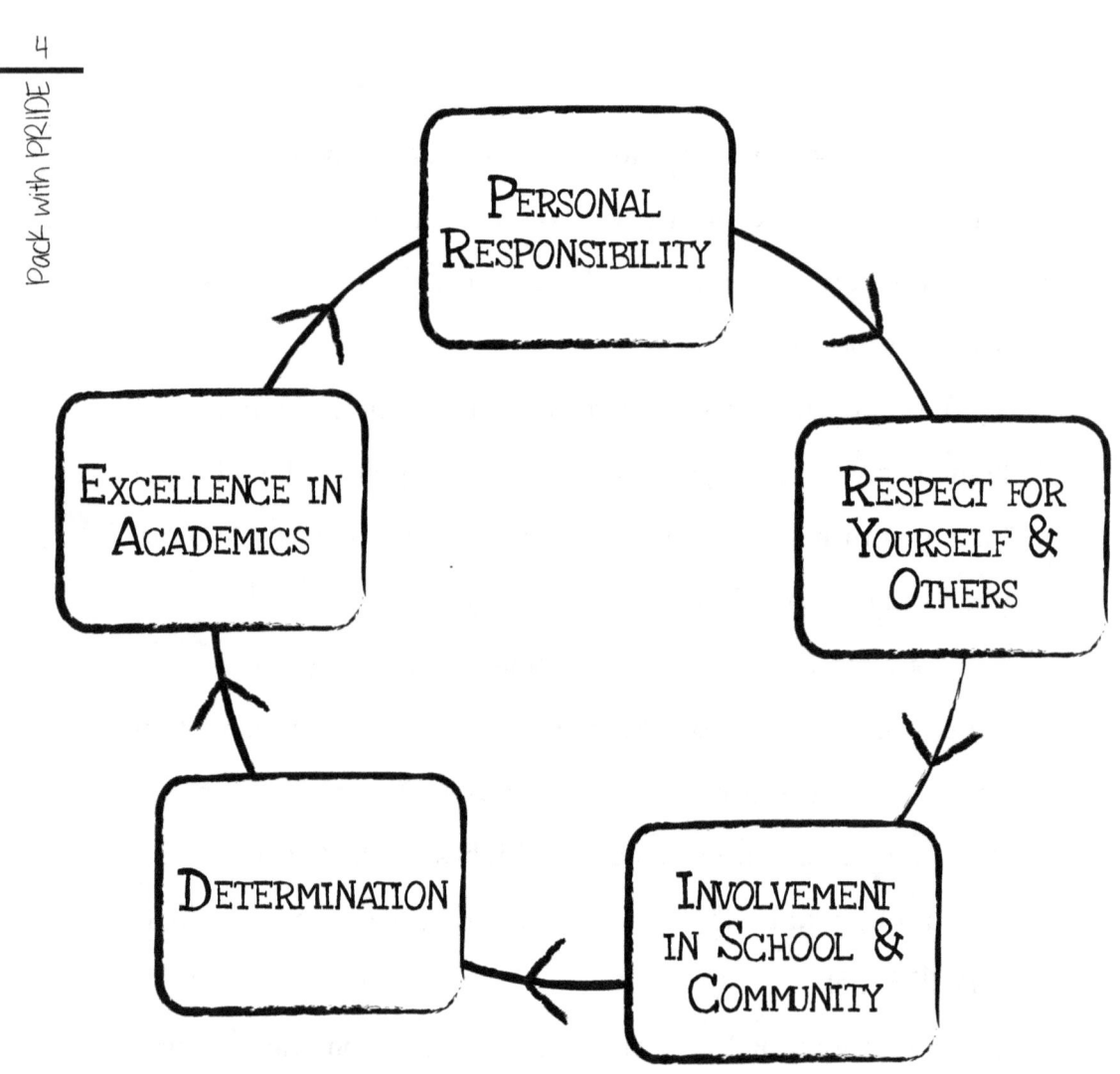

In *Packing Tools for Success Beyond Middle School*, I use PRIDE as an acronym to represent the following tools: Personal Responsibility, Respect, Involvement, Determination, and Excellence. By using these tools, you will set yourself up for a successful and exciting future. In fact, I believe they can help you do, become, and have almost anything you want in life.

Even though my parents only had a sixth grade education, they wanted us to take pride in our home and school work. They knew that doing so was essential to my success. Similarly, my teachers were always saying, "Is this the best you can do?" or, "I know you can do better."

Another way to understand pride is to "do your best" at whatever you are asked to do... your very best.

I am writing this book because I want *you* to be a successful student now and in high school. The PRIDE tools became my friends in middle school, and I am still using them forty years later in my job, with my family, and in the community.

I encourage you to pack these PRIDE tools with you on your middle school journey to ensure success now, in high school, and beyond. I hope you enjoy reading this short book and will share it with a friend.

"I do think that the greatest lesson of life is that you are responsible for your own life."
-Oprah Winfrey

Personal Responsibility

It has been many years since I was in middle school, but I still remember that in the sixth grade I had difficulty telling time. Don't ask me why. For some reason, I had a mental block. It was easier to have my big brother or sister tell me the time or to ask my friends what the time was.

My teacher realized I struggled with knowing how to tell time. She informed my mother that I would have to stay after school for an entire week for special lessons on how to tell time. What an embarrassment! My mother and the teacher explained that no one could study for me. I would have to practice and decide for myself if I wanted to learn how to tell time.

It was then I realized personal responsibility means making choices by myself in challenging situations. My fear that I would look stupid kept me from learning how to tell time. I overcame that fear by simply asking my teacher questions. She was so sweet and helpful. I felt so silly for not asking those questions earlier. Later, I asked myself, "Why did I wait so long to ask for help?"

Pack with PRIDE | 8

> **PERSONAL RESPONSIBILITY**

> **YOUR CHOICE**

> **CHOOSE WISELY**

The first "P" in PRIDE represents Personal Responsibility. A key ingredient in personal responsibility is making wise choices. Middle school is a time in which you want to be popular with your friends and don't want them to see your weaknesses. I had to learn that successful students choose to ask questions when they don't understand the subject.

Taking personal responsibility means making choices in challenging situations.

In middle school you will have to make many choices. Some of the choices you make will not be popular with your friends. Your friends may want you to talk on the phone when you should be doing your homework. You may want to watch your favorite show on TV or go to the movies with friends when you should be working on a project. Will you be strong enough to say, "No"? Start today by making wise choices and using your study time wisely. You are the only one who can determine how far you go in achieving your academic goals.

Did I learn how to tell time? Yes, I did! I decided that telling time was important enough to me and I was in charge of making it happen.

"Never dull your shine
for somebody else."
-Tyra Banks

Respect for Yourself & Others

In the previous chapter, you read about taking responsibility and making wise choices. This section is on "Respect," respect for yourself and others.

You may be thinking, "What does respect have to do with being successful?" Research indicates that if you feel good about yourself, you will have a better attitude about attending school and doing well in your classes.

When is the last time you looked at yourself in the mirror? Did you like what you saw? Have you been kind to someone lately? Many times teens will say unkind words to other classmates because they don't feel good about themselves. Developing a good self-esteem* or self-concept is vital to your success and happiness.

Your middle school years are a time to examine your "core beliefs." You will be refining what your parents taught you and deciding what you believe. Sometimes, students get all caught up in what Albert Ellis calls, "the curse of stinkin' thinkin'." Ellis says stinkin' thinkin' isn't based on reality. Students may think that they are dumb, selfish, a failure, unattractive, or not college material. These self-defeating thoughts can lead to a poor self-esteem—even when they aren't true! Having a poor self-esteem may lead to disrespect towards self and others.

What can you do to ward off stinkin' thinkin'?

- Tell yourself that you deserve to be successful and you *can* do the work.

- Look for and do random acts of kindness. The golden rule is still golden: "Do unto others as you would have them to do unto you." When you start to focus on others rather than yourself, it changes your outlook, and you start thinking like a successful student.

- Choose to rise above negative thoughts from the past that you may have received from friends, parents, or teachers. Instead of listening to your inner critic, develop positive mental images of yourself going to high school and college.

Virginia Satir states, "If your images are positive, they will support you and cheer you on when you get discouraged. Negative pictures rattle around inside of you, affecting you without your knowing it."

---

*"Self-esteem can be defined as the state that exists when you are not arbitrarily haranguing and abusing yourself by choosing to fight back against those automatic thoughts with meaningful rational responses."
—Dr. Thomas Burns

A healthy self-respect leads to self-love. Believe it or not, your academic intelligence has a lot to do with loving and believing in yourself.

"Positive thinking won't let you do anything but it will let you do everything better than negative thinking will."
-Zig Ziglar

Now that you are all pumped up and like what you see in the mirror, it is time to put your thoughts into action. The next chapter is about being getting involved in school and community activities.

"Alone we can
do so little.
Together we can
do so much."
-Helen Keller

Involvement in School & Community

I attended Maggie B. Hudson Junior High School in Longview, Texas. It was only three blocks up the road from my house. All the neighborhood kids walked to school. I enjoyed middle school. I had many good friends and could not wait to get to my classes. We had excellent teachers and a couple of them also belonged to the same church I attended. My teachers were always telling me to work hard because they saw potential in me; I developed great study habits so as to not disappoint them.

We were able to tell it was almost time for lunch by the smell of fresh homemade rolls. The cafeteria workers all wore white uniforms with white shoes. They cooked homemade meals every day. You could tell that the ladies took a great deal of pride in their cooking. We entered the lunch line with great anticipation of enjoying a wonderful meal.

However, in the late 1960s, my landscape changed when the Longview Independent School District was mandated to integrate all of its schools. There would no longer be all black or all white schools. The District gave us a choice. We could voluntarily attend Longview High in 1968 or be mandated to attend the following year. This was a hard decision to make and a very difficult time for our parents, the students (black and white) and the entire community. Consequently, my parents let me decide. I did not know, at the time, what an important decision it would be. I decided to leave my all black high school and attend Longview High School much earlier than the courts required.

This brings us to the letter "I" in PRIDE—Involvement. Involvement was the reason I decided to leave my old high school and enroll in Longview High. I will confess here that I was afraid to go; I was popular at the middle school. But I wanted to get involved in school activities that could help me reach my goal of being a teacher. I guess you could say I wanted to prove to myself and the world that I could stand shoulder to shoulder with anyone—black or white.

I developed a strong self-esteem and believed I was smart. I pictured myself walking across the stage with my diploma. I visualized the yearbook and wondered if there would be commas behind my name. The commas represented the other page numbers on which a student could find his or her picture. Yes, I had many commas behind my name because I became involved in school activities and made many new friends. Some of my teachers were surprised by my persistence to be successful in my studies.

Sean Covey talks about synergy in his book, *The 7 Habits of Highly Effective Teens*. Synergy, simply stated, is the energy created when two or more people work together to create a better solution that they would not be able to create working alone. Synergy is ineffective without "Involvement."

Get involved in your family, church, and community.

Packing the PRIDE tool of being involved in your school and extracurricular activities can promote success in learning. Students who are involved in their church, school, and community have a higher self-esteem and make better grades. You can join a study group, or sign up for a club or sport. I am sure there are several opportunities for involvement in your school. Also, try to find time to volunteer in the community or at your church. You are not too young to help others.

Packing the PRIDE tool of being involved in your school and extra-curricular activities can promote success in your learning. The next section can be a little more challenging for us all. The "D" in PRIDE represents "Determination." Are you ready to read about being a "Determined" student? If so, turn the page and let's pack another PRIDE tool.

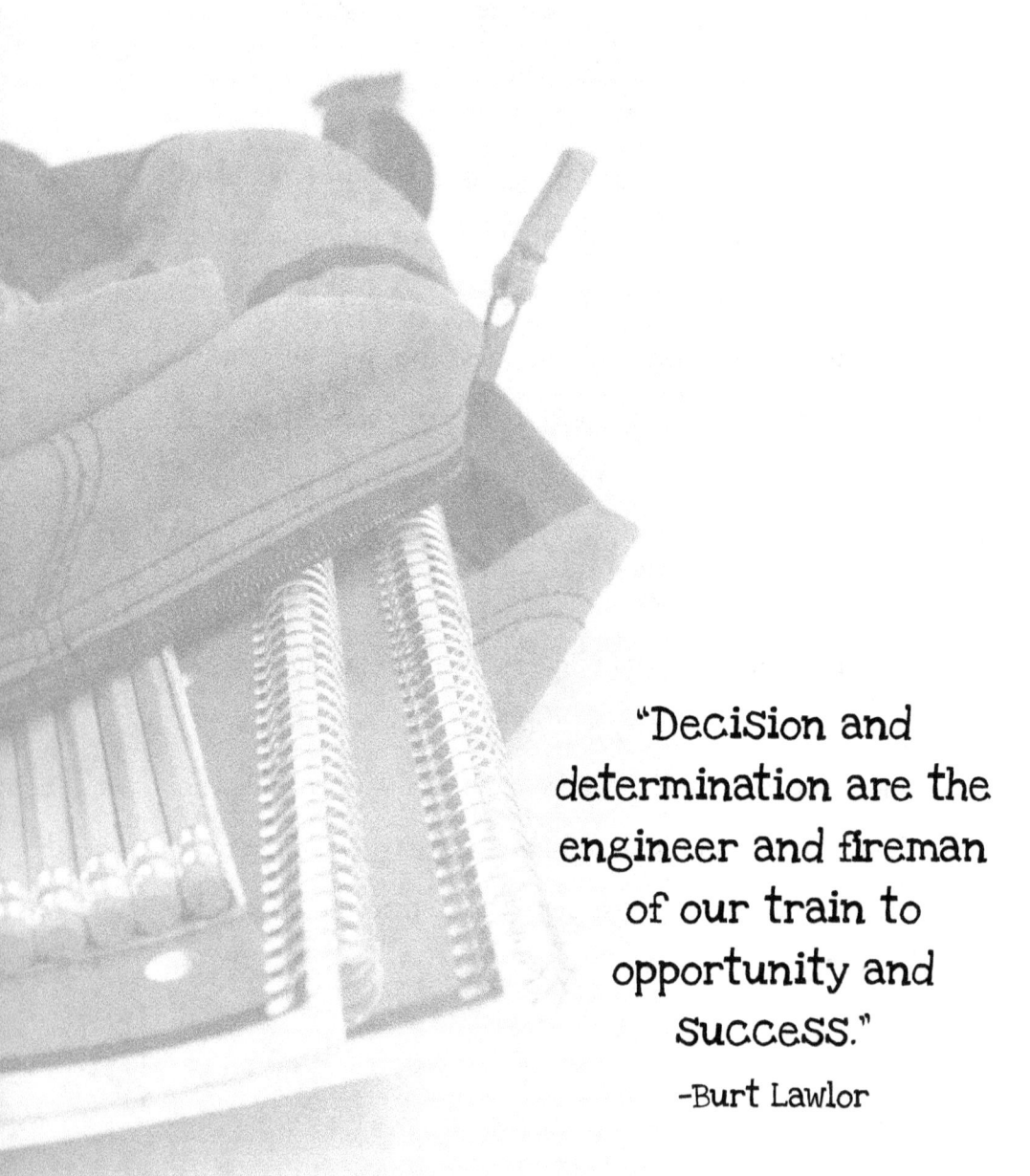

"Decision and determination are the engineer and fireman of our train to opportunity and success."
—Burt Lawlor

Determination

What words come to your mind when you think of "determination?" I think of grit, willpower, resolve, and fortitude. Let me share a parable with you from Skip Downing's teaching guide, *On Course*. It's called, "The Crow and the Pitcher." (A parable is simply a short fable with a purpose of teaching a lesson.) Read the story below carefully to see how determined the crow was in his quest for water.

A crow, exhausted and dying of thirst, came upon a pitcher with water in the bottom; but when the crow put its beak into the mouth of the pitcher, he found that, no matter how hard he tried, he could not reach far enough to drink. He tried for five minutes, almost giving up in despair. But, continuing to think of other options, a creative thought came to him. He took a pebble and dropped it into the pitcher. He repeated the process, dropping in one pebble after another. At last, he saw the water level rising, and after casting in a few more pebbles, he was able to quench his thirst and save his life.

This is a simple parable, but it has a powerful message. When you are faced with a challenging problem or task, don't give in so easily. You must buckle down and have grit and persistence. The crow didn't say, "Oh well, I guess it is my time to die." No. The crow immediately began to come up with creative ideas on how to quench his thirst. He was determined to survive. Think of the crow when you are facing a challenge—in math, science, English or whatever the course may be. Stay with the problem until you devise a solution. Give yourself credit for being able to think of possible solutions.

Success is a good feeling. However, if you are failing or don't understand something, don't be afraid to seek help. The key here is to be persistent and dedicated to completing the assigned task.

Middle school is like a marathon. You have a schedule for each semester with classes to take. Some classes are mandatory and some you can choose by yourself. Before moving to the next level, all courses have to be completed. In running a race, you cannot run one lap, take a break and pick up in the fifth or sixth lap. You have to continue on your path avoiding the potholes one lap after another, one semester after another. A pothole in middle school is any barrier that could impede your studying and classroom participation for success. Let's stop for a moment to talk about some potholes that could interfere with your "PRIDE" tool of Determination.

Procrastination

Procrastination is a big pothole. I tell my students that procrastination and penalties are friends—and they are not friends you want in your circle.

> Procrastination is a pothole you want to avoid.

Procrastination means avoiding beginning or finishing an assignment. Often times when students are not interested in an assignment, they set it aside. Maybe you have done this before, choosing to work on an assignment that was less challenging or more fun. However, what usually happens when you procrastinate, is that you end up not doing the assignment or you turn it in late. *If* you are allowed to turn in a late paper in high school or college, points will certainly be deducted.

Procrastination causes students to become unfocused and lose their determination to finish or turn in the assignment. As a result, they are disappointed in their grades and in themselves. Procrastination is a pothole you want to avoid now and in the future. Use your planner to work ahead so you will not be stressed to rush through an assignment.

Disorganization

Another pothole to avoid is disorganization. Having a well-organized notebook and keeping up with your assignments is a must. Great organizational skills can help you succeed in school.

Dr. Jennifer Hurd, in her textbook *Campus Companion*, lists several tips from the Student Advisory Board for keeping up with assignments. Even though these were written for college students, they are great tips to follow in preparation for high school as well.

Tips for Staying Organized at School

1. If you don't understand an assignment, ask your teacher for help or clarification.
2. Write your assignments in your planner when they are assigned.
3. Divide large projects into smaller, achievable assignments.
4. Organize your notes and assignments in notebooks. A notebook for each class will help you maintain a sense of organization.
5. Set aside a certain period of time each day or evening for study.
6. Make a list of tasks to be done to complete assignments, prioritize these tasks.
7. Planning ahead is best. When you know you'll have a few things due after the weekend, plan to at least start some of them before the weekend rolls around.

Sally Lipsky, in her book, *College Study, The Essential Ingredients*, explains that organization is a vital component of effective, efficient study. When you organize your environment, you create an important sense of self-control and self-management, reducing your levels of anxiety and stress. I believe this is very applicable to middle school students as well.

I have only mentioned a few potholes for you to avoid that will lead you off course—procrastination and disorganization. I am sure you can list others. Remember, successful students are determined and dedicated; they take pride in a job well done.

Last but not least, the final PRIDE tool I want you to pack begins with the letter "E." Yes, you may have already guessed that the "E" in PRIDE stands for "Excellence." I want you to excel in your academics. Are you ready to be an excellent student? Good. Turn the page.

"We are what we
repeatedly do.
Excellence, then,
is not an act,
but a habit."
-Aristotle

Excellence in Academics

Our backpack cannot be complete without the PRIDE tool of "Excellence." Succeeding in middle school (and beyond) requires a commitment to excellence. Do you have to earn all A's? No. It may not be possible to make all A's. However, there is one thing I know for sure: It is possible for you to strive to do your very best in all of your classes.

You will have classes you love and enjoy. It will not be difficult to tackle the homework for those classes. But, for the classes you don't have much interest in, you'll have to motivate yourself. Tell yourself that these courses are important. Eliminate the phrase, "This is good enough." *Is it good enough? Is it really your best work?* Ask yourself these questions before you turn in an assignment in any class. Former Secretary of State Colin Powell said, "There are no secrets to success. It is the result of preparation, hard work, learning from failure." That's a commitment to excellence!

I am reminded of another parable in which a couple hired a builder to build a house. Let's call the couple Mr. and Mrs. Brick, and we will call the builder Bob. The Bricks loved and trusted Bob because of previous jobs he had completed for them.

Bob was excited about building the Bricks' home and immediately began to work on the project. Nevertheless, he became distracted. He spent more time going to movies, eating out, and spending time on Facebook than he did working on

> "There are no secrets to success. It is the result of preparation, hard work, learning from failure."
> –Colin Powell

the Bricks' home. At the end of the day, he rushed over to work on the house. Soon, he began cutting corners and using inferior supplies. As the deadline approached, Bob quickly and sloppily finished the project.

Why did Bob suddenly decide to work at a level that was below his best? We are not sure, especially since the Bricks were his favorite clients. They trusted him and believed he was an honest man who always did quality work.

Bob finished the house. But before the Bricks were able to move in, an unfortunate thing happened to Bob and his family. Bob's house caught on fire and was completely destroyed. He and his family were safe but dazed.

Since the Bricks were quite fond of Bob, and in no hurry to move, they decided to give Bob a gift. Bob thought the gift would be money. Much to his surprise they gave him a set of keys to the house he had built for them. Bob broke down and cried. The Bricks thought his tears were because he was touched by their generous gift, but you and I know better.

Bob knew he had built an inferior house with second-rate supplies. He had not done his best work. Suddenly, he was the one who had to live in the house he thought he was building for the Bricks.

What is the message for you? Always display excellence in whatever you do. This means putting forth your best effort—whether or not you will receive a grade. Don't wait until you get to high school to say, "I wish I had participated in that club," or "I wish I had taken that Spanish course more seriously." Don't avoid taking a class because your best friend said it was too hard. Showing excellence in your studies and taking time to do your very best is a much-desired trait.

- Make it a habit to take your time to study for your assignments.
- Make it a habit to ask questions if you do not understand something.
- Make it a habit to give yourself a learning assignment even if you don't have homework.
- Make it a habit to limit your time on Facebook, playing Internet games, and watching TV.

Remember, you are building your foundation for high school and will have to live in the house (academics) that YOU have built. So, build wisely.

"Always bear in mind that your own resolution to succeed is more important than any one thing."
-Abraham Lincoln

PRIDE On!

When I began writing this book, I had just completed an intense, four-day On Course Workshop in Baltimore, Maryland, led by Skip Downing. The entire workshop focused on active learning strategies to empower students to become responsible learners. At the end of the seminar, we were asked to list professional and personal commitments as a result of this workshop. I pondered for many moments and reflected upon my successes as a wife, mother, grandmother, professor, professional presenter, mentor, and the other roles I serve. There was no doubt in my mind that I should begin writing, *Packing Tools for Success Beyond Middle School*. Even though the workshop was geared for learning and practicing successful strategies for college and university students, the concepts are certainly applicable for middle school success.

Middle school is a fun time. You will not have an opportunity to repeat these years. They go by so fast! I want you to enjoy every moment as you move from semester to semester making new discoveries and developing your career interests.

I don't know where you are on your journey in middle school. You may be in the 5th, 6th, 7th, or 8th grade. Whatever grade you are in, commit to using these PRIDE tools to build a strong foundation for high school and college. Success does not magically happen. There is no shot or pill to take. You must make wise choices and participate actively in your learning. Marian Wright Edelman makes a great point about learning. In her book, *The Measure of Our Success: A Letter to My Children and Yours*, she says you should never stop learning and improving your mind. If you do, you're going to get left behind. The world is changing like a kaleidoscope right before our eyes. Getting the right education will equip you to thrive in your future career. College pays and is a fine investment. What you do right now can help you get into the school of your choice later!

When you pack the tools of PRIDE—Personal Responsibility, Respect for yourself and others, Involvement in school and the community, Determination, and Excellence in academics—you are on your way to becoming a successful student. Your PRIDE tools of success will help you lay a strong foundation for high school and beyond. They have been a part of my life for many years. And now, I am happy to share them with you, so that your academic journey will be successful.

Have a great middle school experience! Remember the quote by Abraham Lincoln, "Always bear in mind that your own resolution to succeed is more important than any one thing."

PRIDE *On!*

THE END...

OR IS IT THE BEGINNING?

Journal Reflections

Journal Reflection #1

Successful students have balcony people or cheerleaders in their lives who motivate them to do their best. List three positive adults in your life (outside of school) that are your balcony people. Write a sentence or two about how they encourage you.

Journal Reflection #2

Reading, writing, and math are basic skills that will serve you well in high school, college, and in your career. What can you do outside of school to boost your strength in these skills?

Journal Reflections

Journal Reflection #3

When you show respect to others at school, home, church, or in the community, what does this say about you?

Journal Reflections

Journal Reflection #4

How old will you be in twenty years? Close your eyes and dream with me. Pretend you are looking through a set of binoculars into the future. What do you see yourself doing? Where are you working? Where do you live? What kind of car do you drive? How do you feel about yourself?

Journal Reflections

Journal Reflection #5

Think about your future career. What volunteer activities can you do to learn more about this career?

Journal Reflections

Journal Reflection #6

Set a short-term goal for this semester. A goal should follow the DAPPS rule. A goal must be **dated** (have a specific deadline), and be **achievable** (realistic, you are able to do it), **personal** (your goal), **positive** (something you want to do) and **specific** (what will you actually do?).

Write your goal below and fill in the answers to make sure it follows the DAPPS rule.

My Goal:

Date by which I will complete this goal:

I can achieve this goal by doing or being:

This goal is personal (not something someone else told me I should do).

☐ Yes ☐ No

Is this something I want to do, be, or have? (Make your goal positive rather than stating what you don't want.)

☐ Yes ☐ No

Is this goal specific? (Don't say I want to get better grades. Decide what specific grade you want to earn.)

Journal Reflection #7

After reading, *Packing Tools for Success Beyond Middle School*, what changes do you need to make to prepare for success in high school?

Journal Reflections

My Motivational Quotes for Success

I've left space on the next few pages for you to write down some of your favorite quotes—words that motivate and inspire you to be your best. The pages are designed so that you can cut out your quotes and put them where you'll see them every day. Tape them to your bathroom mirror, on your school folders, or on the inside of your locker door.

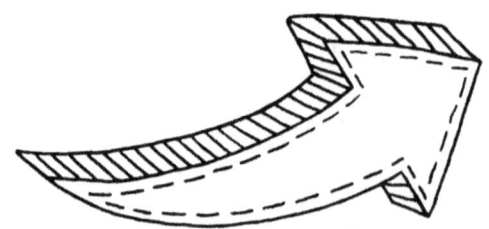

"At the end of the day, what you have inside is much more beautiful than what's on the outside!"
-Selena Gomez

"You can have an impact anywhere you are."
—Tony Dungy

"Nothing is impossible;
the word itself says 'I'm possible!'"
-Audrey Hepburn

"Once a commitment is made,
without the option of backing out,
the mind releases tremendous energy
toward its achievement."
-Ben Dominitz

My Contract for Academic Success

My name is _____ and I am in the ____ grade. I attend _____ (school). I commit to attend class, be on time, participate in class, show respect to my fellow classmates, parents and adults. I understand that it is important that I complete my assignments (by myself) before spending time watching TV, playing video games, connecting on Facebook, or surfing the Internet. If I do not understand something in class, I will ask the teacher for further explanation. I also understand that it is very important that I apply myself in class to have a strong foundation to prepare for high school. I will move out of my comfort zone to take challenging courses that may appear to be hard. I will have a positive attitude and I will set goals to fulfill this commitment. I will be a dependable, honest, persistent student as I know these are traits that will improve my life now and in the future.

Date: _____

Adult Witness: _____

Your Printed Name: _____

Your Signature: _____

REFERENCES

Covey, Sean. *The 7 Habits of Highly Effective TEENS.*
    © 1998 by Franklin Covey Co.

Downing, Skip. *On Course: Strategies for Creating Success in College and in Life.*
    © 2011 by Wadsworth, Cengage Learning.

Edelman, Marian Wright. *The Measure of Our Success.*
    © 1992 by Marian Wright Edelman.

Forbes Leadership Library. *Thoughts on Success.*
    © 1995 by Forbes Inc.

Hurd, Jennifer. *Campus Companion.*
    © 2007 by Houghton Mifflin Company.

Lipsky, Sally A. *College Study, The Essential Ingredients.*
    © 2008, 2004 by Pearson Education, Inc.

About the Author

Essie Childers, M. Ed.
*President and Founder, Mvita Consulting
Founder and Director, Young Ladies Success Seminar*

Essie Childers graduated from Abilene Christian University with a bachelor's degree in education and with a master's in reading from The University of Texas at Tyler. Essie is a full-time professor for Blinn College in Bryan, Texas, teaching student success courses and reading. She married her college sweetheart, Terry, and has three wonderful children and two sweet grandchildren. Essie's passion is encouraging students, educators, and community leaders to strive for excellence and visualize success in every task. She offers engaging, active learning workshops for educators, parents, schools, and community groups. Some of Essie's favorite activities include going to the movies, baking, missionary work, conference presentations, and taking vacations with her family.

www.ingramcontent.com/pod-product-compliance
Lightning Source LLC
Chambersburg PA
CBHW051215290426

44109CB00021B/2459